For Rene
Alaska Bedtime Rhymes...
sweet dreams

Mark Kelley

May 28, 2014

Once Upon Alaska
Alaska
A Kid's Photo Book

Photography by Mark Kelley

Rhyming Verse by Nick Jans

PHOTOGRAPHY
MARK KELLEY

Publisher: Mark Kelley
Photographer: Mark Kelley
Writer: Nick Jans
Designer: Heidi Reifenstein
Digital Imaging Specialist: Terra Dawn Parker
Consultants: Linda Torgerson and Malou Peabody
A Special Thanks to Larry Persily and Rich Peabody
Proofreader: Tina Brown
Printer: Samhwa Printing, Co., Ltd., Seoul, South Korea
Print Broker: Alaska Print Brokers, Anchorage, Alaska

Mailing Address: Mark Kelley / PO Box 20470 / Juneau, AK 99802 / USA
Business Phone: (907) 586-1993 or Toll Free: (888) 933-1993
FAX Number: (907) 586-1201
Email: photos@markkelley.com
Website: www.markkelley.com

Copies of "Once Upon Alaska" can be ordered by calling Mark Kelley or
going to the website at www.markkelley.com

First Printing: December 2013
10 9 8 7 6 5 4 3 2 1

ISBN-13: 978-1-88086-520-0

DEDICATED TO
Jan, Gabe and Owen
"For the child in all of us"

A land so  so grand and wide and far

We came to visit—
here we are!

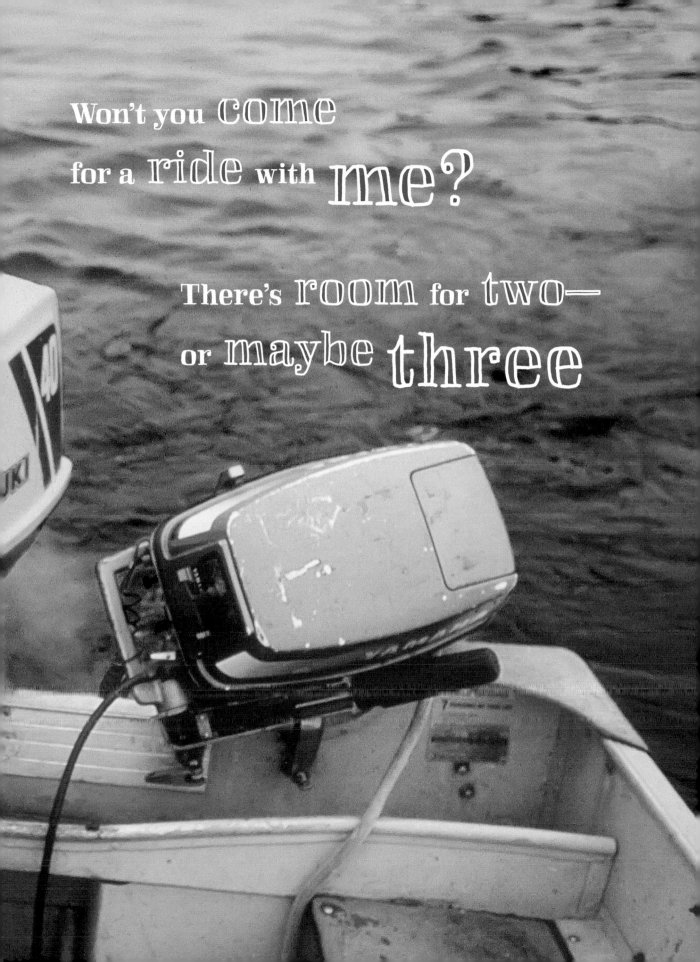

Won't you come
for a ride with me?

There's room for two—
or maybe three

In the breath between storms, light paints the sky

Rainbow glows
and the boat glides by

Fins a-shimmer, tails a-shiver

Wriggling up the icy river

I dream a dream upon the sea

To catch a fish
as big as me

With a **crash**
and a **splash**
I raise my **tail**

To the **roving** life
of a **humpback**
whale

A Whoosh and an Ahhh...
mouths open wide

A thousand herring scooped inside

Sea and sky
become the **same**

Orca's breath
a silver **flame**

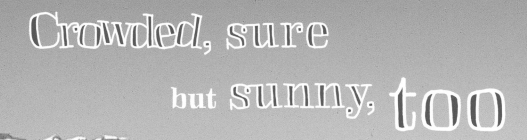

Crowded, sure
but sunny, too

There's room for me
but not for you

A little snooze
upon the water

Just the way
an otter oughter

We don't mind
a bed of ice

But a **comfy mattress**

might be **nice**

Glacier growls
and creaks
and rumbles

Down its
face blue
boulder
tumbles

Great river of ice
flows through the land

Carving peaks with icy hand

A world of ice,
A world of snow

A plane up high
with far to go

Swooping low
to snatch a meal

With golden beak
and claws of steel

Mom said, "woof" and here we are

We hope she didn't go too far

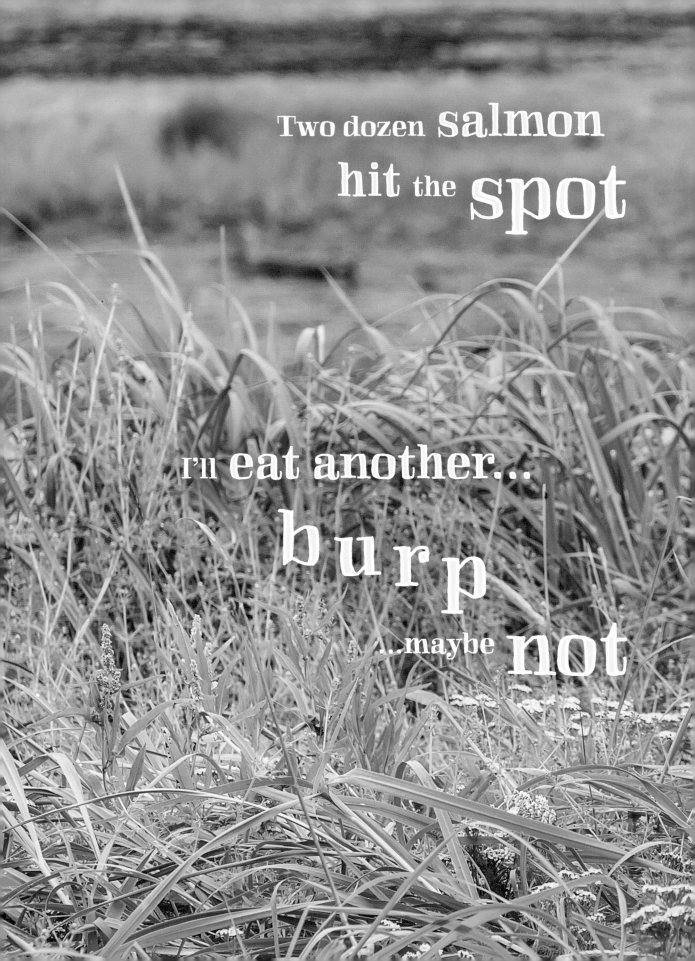

Two dozen salmon
hit the spot

I'll eat another...
burp
...maybe not

No need to stare—
please look away

It's just another
bad hair day

Mom keeps me safe
on mountain high

Above the clouds
where eagles fly

My time is marked by amber horn

A curl that grew
since I was born

Big but gentle,
strong but shy

I'll wait right here
till you pass by

My grandma pumped
her water here

It tastes the same,
so pure and clear

Ancient faces
carved in
wood

Would whisper
stories if they
could

Mountains glow
with pale green light

Aurora dances in the night

Alaska Fun & Factoids

A cow moose and calf stand silhouetted in Wonder Lake, at the end of the road in Denali National Park. Behind them rises 20,000-foot Mount McKinley, the tallest mountain in North America. The Koyukon Indian name for the mountain is Denali, which means The High One.

This is Mark's son, Gabe, years ago. Kids from smaller, roadless Southeast Alaska coastal towns like Pelican and Tenakee Springs grow up with their hand around an outboard motor tiller, and as teenagers, look forward to getting a boat instead of a car.

Alaska's commercial fishing industry is one of the richest in the world, providing nearly 80,000 jobs to the state economy. And, as dramatized on the reality TV series, *Deadliest Catch*, fishing is also one of Alaska's most dangerous jobs.

Pink salmon, also called humpies, swim up the fish ladder at Douglas Island Pink and Chum (DIPAC) fish hatchery in Juneau. There are five species of salmon in Alaska, and each species has two names: 1) king/chinook; 2) silver/coho; 3) chum/dog; 4) sockeye/red; and 5) pink/humpies.

Mark's son, Owen, poses with a king salmon his mother caught. While a very nice fish, it's far from the record book. The largest king salmon ever caught weighed over 100 pounds, and 50 pounders (about double the size of this fish) are caught every year.

Humpback whales are the most common large whale in coastal Alaska waters. They are also the most acrobatic, and sometimes breach (jump) completely clear of the water. Humpbacks commonly reach 40 feet—the length of a school bus—and their tails are 12 to 15 feet across.

These **humpback whales** are engaged in a spectacular feeding activity known as bubble netting. Working together, a group of whales uses exhaled bubbles to herd schools of bait fish toward the surface, and then the whales lunge through the mass, mouths wide open. Sea water is strained out through rows of baleen, leaving behind a huge mouthful of wriggling fish. Rare elsewhere in the world, bubble netting is fairly common in Southeast Alaska.

Like **all sea mammals,** orcas (also known as killer whales) need to breathe, just as we do. Their dives last anywhere from three to five minutes. The deepest recorded dive for an orca was over 900 feet. Scientists recognize at least two types of orcas: fish-eating "residents," and sea-mammal eating "transients." Their behaviors are different, and they speak different "languages."

While **similar in** appearance to harbor seals, Steller sea lions are much larger. A big male can weigh close to a ton, and reach 10 feet in length. Sea lions often "haul out" on navigation buoys like this one, and their growls, groans, and roars may be heard from up to a mile away.

Glaciers **that meet the** sea are known as tidewater glaciers. As these massive rivers of ice flow downhill, their faces are undercut by tidal currents, resulting in spectacular "calving" as huge chunks of ice break off. The faces of some glaciers reach more than 200 feet into the air, and may extend farther than that underwater.

Sea **otters are large** members of the weasel family. They have the densest hair of any mammal, up to one million hairs per square inch. In between diving for crabs, sea urchins, and other shellfish, they rest on their backs on the surface, paws out of the water to conserve body heat, and groom their fur.

Drifting **icebergs near** the face of tidewater glaciers serve as nurseries for harbor seal mothers and their pups. The ice offers a place to rest and sun, as well as refuge from their main predator, the orca (also known as killer whale).

Margerie Glacier is a tidewater glacier located deep inside Glacier Bay National Park and Preserve, and can only be reached by plane or boat. In the photo the ice above the water is 25 stories high. The additional ice below the water is about 10 stories high. Together the total face, or terminus, of the glacier is higher than the Statue of Liberty.

More than 80 miles long and nearly 50 miles wide, the Juneau Icefield is larger than the state of Rhode Island. It holds almost forty large valley glaciers and over 100 smaller ones. Tens of thousands of people visit the icefield each year.

Bald eagles are born brown, and stay that way until they reach adulthood, around age five. Then the young birds' brown head and tail feathers turn their distinctive white. There are more bald eagles in Alaska—well over 30,000—than in the rest of the whole world.

Unlike larger brown/grizzly bears, black bears are agile climbers. Mothers often park their cubs high in trees where they are safe from large male bears. Their typically dark color helps them blend into the forest shadows. Though they are called black these bears may be cinnamon colored, blue-gray, or even cream colored.

In late summer and into autumn, brown bears eat almost constantly, building up fat for winter hibernation. When the fishing is good, a bear may catch more than 50 salmon a day. Favorite parts are the fatty skin, the eggs, and the heads.

A porcupine has over a quarter of a million quills, and it is born with them all. A porcupine cannot throw its quills; when frightened, this peaceful, slow-moving member of the rodent family swats with its broad tail to protect itself. A baby porcupine is known as a porcupette.

Mountain goats (pictured here) and Dall sheep (below) are two different but similar species, both whitish in color. Goats live in warmer, wetter coastal mountains along the Southeastern edge of Alaska, and have shaggy coats and black dagger-shaped horns; Dall sheep inhabit mountains of the colder, drier Interior of Alaska.

A male Dall sheep's age can be read by examining its horns. Each growth year is marked by a band, most clearly seen on the back of a horn. A Dall sheep can live to be a dozen or more years old, and judging from its horns, this big ram is at least ten.

The moose is the largest member of the deer family. Only the males have antlers. Despite their fierce reputation, they are usually quiet and peaceful, and may live in suburban backyards in Alaska cities. The odd, dangling fold of skin on its neck is called a dewlap, or bell. Its exact function is unknown, but it may serve to help transfer the animal's scent.

While most Alaskans live in larger cities with modern conveniences, many residents of smaller towns still enjoy a rustic lifestyle that seems from another time. Here, a girl pumps a drink at her family cabin in Gustavus, in Southeast Alaska.

Totem poles are made only by Tlingit, Haida, and Tsimshian people of the Pacific Northwest and Southeast Alaska. Carved from rot-resistant yellow cedar, totem poles are erected for a variety of purposes: to display clan crests, to commemorate an event or individual, or even to ridicule someone (a so-called "shame pole").

The scientific name for the northern lights is Aurora Borealis. They are caused by bursts of electrically charged particles streaming off the sun (so-called solar winds) that strike the earth's upper atmosphere. The most common shades range from pale to yellowish green, but they may be vivid green, purple, or red.

Alaska kids
know how to swing

A fishing buoy's
just the thing